EMBRACING the SOJOURNERS

EMBRACING the SOJOURNERS

The church's ministry to migrant families through Head Start, child care

Charles Edmond Barnes, D.Min.
United Theological Seminary, 1993

ST. LOUIS, MISSOURI

Copyright @1993 by Charles Edmond Barnes. Republished in 2020. All rights reserved. For information about reproducing any material, email barnes73@twc.com

ISBN: 9781603500890

Published by Lucas Park Books

www.lucasparkbooks.com

Printed in the United States of America

UNITED THEOLOGICAL SEMINARY

THE CHURCH's MINISTRY TO MIGRANT FAMILIES THROUGH HEAD START CHILD CARE

A FINAL DOCUMENT SUBMITTED TO
THE DOCTOR OF MINISTRY PROGRAM COMMITTEE
OF UNITED THEOLOGICAL SEMINARY
IN PARTIAL FULFILLMENT OF THE REQUIREMENTS
FOR THE DEGREE OF DOCTOR OF MINISTRY

BY
CHARLES EDMOND BARNES
GOLDSBORO, NORTH CAROLINA
APRIL, 1993

TABLE OF CONTENTS

ABSTRACT	ix
ACKNOWLEDGMENT	xi
1. INTRODUCTION	1
2. BACKGROUND INFORMATION	3
3. BIBLICAL AND THEOLOGICAL IMPLICATIONS	9
God And Israel, The Sojourners	11
The Bible Speaks About The Poor	12
The Church As A Called Out People	14
4. THE LIFE-STYLE OF A MIGRANT FARMWORKER	23
Who Are These People?	23
The Role Of The Crew Leader/Labor Contractor	29
Health Care Problems Among Migrants	35
Educational Background Of Migrants	41
5. A PASTORAL CARE APPROACH TO MIGRANT MINISTRY	47
6. THE DELEGATE AGENCY	53
7. THE GRANTEE AGENCY	57
8. THE EVALUATION PROCESS	63
9. APPROACHING THE 21ST-CENTURY	65
Decent Housing For Migrants	65
Improvements For The 21st-Century	68
CONCLUSION	71
APPENDIX	73
BIBLIOGRAPHY LIST	77

ABSTRACT

MINISTRY TO MIGRANT FAMILIES THROUGH HEAD START CHILD CARE: A CASE STUDY AT ST. JAMES CHRISTIAN CHURCH OF GOLDSBORO, NC

Charles Edmond Barnes United Theological Seminary, 1993 Mentors:

Dr. Samuel DeWitt Proctor

Dr. Otis Moss, Jr.

This project sought to increase awareness of economic and social injustices that effect migrant families. Using St. James Christian Church as a model, ways were developed for a local church and community to become role models for mission in ministry. Results of the project showed that a church can be an advocate to ensure needed services for migrant farm workers and their families.

ACKNOWLEDGMENT

I am pleased to acknowledge my indebtedness to the many people who made this project possible. Without the support and time which they have given, the completion of this project would have been impossible.

I express my deepest gratitude to my dear wife, Yvonne, who has always offered her support, and has never stopped believing in me. Her expertise and suggestions have been very helpful and are well appreciated. A special thanks is conveyed to my three children, Michael, Charlie, and Cheresa for allowing Dad time away on the weekends. Likewise, I extend my gratitude to my two wonderful sisters-in-law, Lois and Lyola Artis, who have endured many hours of reading and critiquing. Also, I thank my seven associates, Karen Howard, Lois Artis, Angela White, Brenda Jordan, Yvonne Barnes, Mary Ward, and Norberto Serrano, who sacrificed time away from their families.

To the Saint James Christian Church Family, who demonstrated unselfish and kind patience, I express my sincere thanks. I am also indebted to the many kind church friends who understood when I had to refuse their invitations, and I thank my ministerial friends who fulfilled those preaching engagements for me.

In appreciation, I would like to acknowledge Dr. Mardina MacDonald, Assistant Professor and Registrar of Barton College, Wilson, North Carolina, for her extensive library and computer research. Also, I acknowledge Mr. Bill Moore of the Employment Security Commission, Wilson, North Carolina, for data on labor contractors for North Carolina. I acknowledge Dr. David Abalos, a professor of Seton College, New Jersey, for making himself available for biblical research data. In addition, I submit a special and kind thanks to Frances Banks for her computer knowledge and assistance, which alleviated much stress.

The beginning of this "Model in Ministry" project began with the East Coast Migrant Head Start Project, in Arlington, Virginia and two dear friends, Geraldine O'Brien and JoEllen Shannon. These two women continue to have faith in Saint James Christian Church in delivering quality services to migrant families. I extend a very special thanks to the many migrant farmworkers and families who have been the role models for this project.

I stand in fellowship, with gratitude, to my most knowledgeable mentors, Dr. Samuel D. Proctor, and Dr. Otis Moss, Jr., for their guidance and professional leadership.

Finally, I thank God Almighty for giving to humankind the supreme example of love, acceptance, and servanthood – Jesus Christ.

1

INTRODUCTION

The writer is the Senior Pastor of Saint James Christian Church (Disciples of Christ) located in a rural area, Pitt County, North Carolina. Saint James operates two migrant child care centers that have served families and children for twelve years. Drawing upon his experience in this particular ministry, the writer has been led to present the Doctor of Ministry project dealing with, "The Church's Ministry To Migrant Families Through Head Start Child Care."

Twenty-five years ago, Saint James Christian Church was surrounded by sharecropper families. These families did not own their homes and were forced to be bound by the rules of the landowners. The landowners' rules ranged from forced child labor to homelessness at their discretion. Frequently, children incurred extensive, consecutive absences from school and found it difficult to maintain academic success. Often, after excessive absences, children experienced the emotional trauma of embarrassment upon their return to school. This led to a high dropout rate within the rural communities. Many of the young people migrated North to live with relatives; they usually ended up with unskilled jobs that paid minimum wages.

The "Model in Ministry" is a project addressing and serving the needs of migrant children and their families. The purpose of this Project is to show how one church approaches social and economic injustices through providing continuity of Head Start Services to children of migrant farmworkers. For this "Model in Ministry," Saint James Christian Church is expanding its present Head Start operation in order to establish a third center site for additional children. The congregation and the writer's associate team are actively involved in this exciting expansion project which, thus far, has been a rewarding experience for all involved. The writer's research indicates that this process-setting up a Head Start Child Care Center in project design, sets a precedent. Any church or other non-profit organization interested in developing this kind of ministry should find this information helpful as well as instructional.

It is the writer's intent to discuss the biblical and theological implications for the church's social involvement in the community. The writer will present background information, theological support, life-styles and problems of migrants, pastoral care as a solution, a model for social ministry in the twenty-first century and concluding remarks.

2

BACKGROUND INFORMATION

As a child, the writer was forced to work in fields, cropping tobacco and cotton. Working long hours in the sun and being exposed to dangerous farm equipment, the writer experienced personally the problems associated with the use of children as farm laborers. After the completion of high school in 1964, the writer, opting out of farm life, moved to Washington, District of Columbia, and stayed with relatives.

In 1966, the rural community near Fountain, North Carolina experienced a "Black Flight." Many farmworkers, as the writer, left the small community. Although numerous black farmworkers had moved away from the area, Saint James Christian Church remained in Pitt county, only moving less than one half of a mile away from its original location. In spite of the fact that the population of the immediate community had decreased considerably, Saint James continued to serve the community and to seek ways to improve the conditions of people living in the area.

In an effort to respond to the needs of rural families, the Farmers Home Administration (FmHA), *issued* low interest loan *monies* to low income families to build new homes in 1968. There were many families who took advantage of this opportunity, and for the first time, they moved into their own homes. Most of the landowners would not sell land to build these houses. Perhaps it was because they knew that the control over the rural families would become a thing of the past. For many of these families, the landowners no longer dictated their day-to-day activities. During this same period, many textile factories began to move to the Southern States. People no longer had to earn their living by working on the farm. The people either moved closer to their jobs or wherever they could find someone who would sell them a lot of land on which to build their homes. The writer recalls, that over a ten-year period, many people moved away from the Saint James Church community. At least, families could experience some form of independence from the landowners. This left many farmers without workers. Farmers began to turn to out of state workers. This led to the beginning of migrant workers moving up and down the east coast.

Being raised in a rural community, the writer has experienced some of the arduous life-styles of the migrant families. The father, of the writer, died when he was three years old. His mother, a widow, was left with ten children and the responsibilities as head of the household. Late one winter evening in November, the writer recalls a car horn blowing outside of his family's home. His mother went outdoors to talk with her employer. The landowner told his mother that, "he wanted the family to vacate the property no later than the first of January." The writer's mother came back into the house with a depressed look upon her face. She shared the sad news of having to relocate, with her family. The writer was nine years old at this time; he remembers crying from the fear of not having any place to live and from the fear of losing his friends. During his entire public school years, the writer attended four schools and lived in three counties. He experienced migrating with his family from one farm to another. The plight of this family resembles that of the migrant family. Migrant workers do not stay in the same house, community or state, year after year or month after month. Migrants move from state to state or from county to county, picking the food we eat. Their work is essential to the agricultural industry and the economy of the United States. Life as a migrant farmworker is not easy.

Housing and other basic necessities are often minimal. Frequently, migrants are not permitted to participate in local community services because they are transient. Migrants are there when their hands are useful and told to leave when they are no longer needed. Such a life disrupts a family's home and community existence.

Saint James Christian Church (Disciples of Christ), is located in a rural community of Pitt county in eastern North Carolina. The Church is situated twenty-five miles West of Greenville, North Carolina and three miles West of Fountain, North Carolina. This Church was conceived from the vision of two lay brothers. They started a Sunday school in 1917 in an old abandoned church owned by the Reverend Laura Speight. Saint James' original name was Speight's Chapel Church of Christ (Disciples of Christ). The church was affiliated with the Goldsboro-Raleigh Assembly in which a Bishop was overseer of all the churches.

In 1965, the church's name was changed to Saint James Christian Church (Disciples of Christ) and was affiliated with the Christian Church (Disciples of Christ) in the United States and Canada. The membership of the Christian Church in the United States and Canada is eighty percent White. Blacks, Hispanic, Asians and other minorities make up the other 20 percent. At the present, the denomination's membership totals 1.1 million people. Saint James Christian Church is chartered by the Christian Church (Disciples of Christ) in North Carolina. The church is a predominantly Black congregation with one White member and one Hispanic member.

The writer's family attended Saint James Christian Church.

The father, of the writer, had once been a deacon of this church. The writer returned to North Carolina in 1972. He re-established himself in a nearby community. In 1975, the Saint James called the writer, Charles Edmond Barnes, as its fourth pastor. He succeeded his father-in-law who was the pastor of the church for fifteen years.

Outreach ministry has been a constant concern of Saint James Christian Church. Saint James has shared ministry with other churches in "home bound meals" for senior citizens. Each year the church raises money for the Saint Jude Research Children's Hospital. The writer's concept of ministry is broad and includes more than going to church every Sunday for worship. The writer's vision is for a continual ministry in which the church is involved in ministry, daily. There seems to be numerous space in many churches that is used on Sunday, only. This type of situation changed at Saint James Christian Church after the writer attended a workshop on "Federally Funded Programs for Churches." The Senior Pastor left the workshop with the idea of initiating a Head Start Child Care Center.

The Saint James Christian Church Migrant Head Start has been funded by East Coast Migrant Head Start Project since.1979, to provide continuity of Head Start services to migrant children and their families in eastern North Carolina. Saint James is one of four North Carolina Delegate Agencies of the East Coast Migrant Head Start Project located in Arlington, Virginia.

3

BIBLICAL AND THEOLOGICAL IMPLICATIONS

> If a stranger sojourn with thee in your land, ye shall not vex him. But the stranger that dwelleth with you shall be unto you as one born among you, and thou shalt love him as thyself; for ye were strangers in the land of Egypt: I am the Lord your God. (Lev. 19:33-34)

The migrant families, that come to our communities to plant and to harvest the crops, are the "sojourners." In the Law of Moses and later through the prophets, God warned His people that judgment would result from their refusal to show justice to the poor, the oppressed and the powerless.

There is no greater truth in the Old Testament than that of Israel as being God's special people. It is here that God promises ownership of His people. The Scripture makes this to be a basic factor. "You yourselves have seen what I did to the Egyptians, and how I bore you on eagles' wings, and brought you to Myself." (Ex. 19:4 NAS) What God is saying to Israel can be interpreted as His divine will with regard to human dignity and welfare. "...if you will indeed obey My voice and keep My covenant, then you shall be My own possession among all the peoples, for all the earth is Mine." (Ex. 19:5 NAS)

There were three things which God did in making these insignificant people His special people.

1. God loved them. Israel was puzzled as to why God chose it to be His special people. God did not call Israel because it was powerful and strong. Israel was often the smallest of nations. Nor was Israel particularly gifted. It was often spiritually blunt, morally insensitive, and faithless on its commitments to God. Israel was stiff-necked and rebellious. There was only one thing that made any sense out of the puzzle: God loved Israel and had called it in grace.

2. God had redeemed Israel. Its people were helpless slaves in Egypt under the merciless hand of a powerful and ruthless king. Humanly speaking, there was no way of escape. Any kind of rebellion would have been suicide. But God delivered them with the mighty hand and the outstretched arm.•••• (Deut. 26:8 NAS)

3. God had bound these free people to Him in covenant. Before anything else, this covenant was a relationship. But Israel must exercise its freedom responsibly. Therefore, God gave Israel laws which set limits and boundaries beyond which she could not go. It was inside these boundaries that Israel was to find freedom.

God And Israel. The Sojourners

Both in the Law of Moses and later through the prophets, God warned His people that judgment would result from their refusal to show justice to the poor, and to the oppressed, and to the powerless. God delivered Israel from its oppression, and Israel in turn became oppressive. This is what Israel attempted to do. God warned Israel what He expected its behavior to be.

> If a stranger sojourn with thee in your land, ye shall not vex him. But the stranger that dwelleth with you shall be unto you as one born among you, and thou shalt love him as thyself; for Ye were strangers in the land of Egypt: I am the Lord your God. (Lev. 19:33-34)

The writer believes that God is saying to Israel let kindness root itself in generous love. You should act towards strangers as if the service were being rendered unto you. This will teach you how to act, what to do and how to show courtesy. One will never know when he/she may be in the stranger's position. There was a constant temptation for an Israelite to take advantage of a stranger, since the stranger's family was not large or present to give him/her support and protection. Once again Israel was to refuse this temptation in the name of justice and humanity. Two ineradicable facts stood over an Israelite, controlling his way of life: (a). there was a special relationship to God as a member of the covenant people Israel, (b). without the grace of God they would have been a slave in Egypt like their ancestors. Israel must not forget that the call for obedience is without favoritism from God. Obedience was a demand of the law and the assertion of grace that lies behind it. Humankind are not allowed to pick and choose its duty, but must aim at standing complete in all the will of God. God challenged Israel to be in mercy of how He rescued them; they should constrain her to care for others. God's relationship to humankind is for it to illustrate His lovingkindness. God's commands to courtesy cannot be evaded with impunity. "'For I was hungry, and ye gave me no meat: I was thirsty, and ye gave me no drink.'" (Mt. 25:42). We must not forget that when one is ministering to the needy, he/she is ministering also to Christ. When Israel was in Egypt as a slave, it obtained many afflictions from the hand of Pharaoh. But God told Moses, the cry of the children of Israel has come up to me. God heard them groaning, and God remembered his covenant with Abraham, Isaac, and with Jacob. God looked upon the children of Israel, and God had respect unto them.

The Bible Speaks About The Poor

> Blessed be the Lord of Israel, For He has visited us and accomplished redemption. And has raised up a horn of salvation or us..., As He spoke by the mouth of his holy prophets from of old,--Salvation FROM OUR ENEMIES, And FROM THE HAND OF ALL WHO HATE US... (Lk. 1:68-71 NAS)

The news is therefore good news to the people; it is a reason for joy and gladness, since it gives hope of a total change. In Luke's gospel a messenger of the Lord tells the shepherds: "I bring you good news of great joy which will come to all the people." (Lk. 2:10 NAS). The Good News is evidently not so good for some people. King Herod was deeply concerned when they told him that the king of the Jews had been born. We are told that because he feared to lose his throne he ordered the killing of all children in Bethlehem who were less than two years old.

The shepherds, on the other hand, rejoiced when they heard the news. The shepherds were men who lived in the fields and took turns watching over their flocks at night. They enjoyed little respect because they were part of the masses. When they received the good news, they were glad; they listened and shared it with others. The good news that speaks of the liberation of the oppressed cannot be pleasing to the oppressors who want to go on exploiting the poor. But the good news is indeed good to those who want to change and to see a more just society.

For the most part, those who want to live in a society in which justice and peace reign are those who suffer hunger, oppression and poverty. According to Rebecca S. Chopp's book, The Praxis Of Suffering,

> Through the privileged option for the poor and through the root metaphor of God as liberator, Latin American liberation theology elaborates a new understanding of human existence and a new interpretation of Christianity. Its interests are the quest for freedom, equality, and justice on the part of the poor, those who have been continually victimized in history; its concerns are false ideology, structural oppression, human dignity, and a liberating faith.[1]

For this reason the Good News is directed especially to the poor. Jesus himself said when He read from the Book of Isaiah:

> The Spirit of the Lord is upon me, because he has anointed me to preach good news to the poor. He has sent me to proclaim release to the captives and recovering of sight to the blind, to set at liberty those who are oppressed, to proclaim the acceptable year of the Lord. (Lk. 4:18-19 NAS)

---

[1] Rebecca S. Chopp, The Praxis Of Suffering, (Maryknoll, New York: Orbis Books, 1986), 25.

The Church As A Called Out People

The Greek word for church is "ekklesia" a called out people. Christ has called his church into the world to minister to those that make up the hopeless community.

The writer has discovered through various conversations with migrant families that much of the migrant population is rooted in the Catholic religious belief. Upon arrival to North Carolina, many of them become dropouts from church. Many of them do not attend the Catholic church. The majority of the migrant families are Spanish-speaking people. At Saint James, and numerous non- Catholic churches across America, worship services are performed in the English language only. Interpreters are not available. Therefore, migrants will not want to come to our institutional Church Services.

For two years, Saint James opened its doors to a Spanish Sunday church mini try. The Southern Baptist Association region in this area sponsored a bilingual minister to head the mission. The Spanish church discontinued when that particular minister completed seminary. The attendants were few, but the opportunity for worship in a church setting was made available. The writer believes that Saint James Christian Church has been called to minister to migrant families. We know that our church budget of $70,000.00 will not allow us to do this kind of mission ministry on a larger scale. By obtaining a Head Start grant, it has enabled the church to manage and administer a Migrant Head Start Program within its ministry on a broader scale. The writer recalls conversations with his ministerial peers in which he shared his vision of starting a Head Start Child\Care Project. It appeared that his peers were against opening the doors of their churches to the state and federal government. Instead of being concerned about the government, the writer envisioned this as an opportunity for

Saint James Christian Church to widen its mission ministry. The Bible teaches that, "THE EARTH is the Lord's and all it contains, The world, and those who dwell in it.:" (Ps. 24:1 NAS) This was another opportunity for the church to witness to a broken humanity. Doctor Samuel D. Proctor in his book Samuel Proctor: My Moral Odyssey, says,

> My world began to widen. My wife and our two sons agreed to go also, and their world widened, too. My sons Herb and Tim integrated a "white" school in Nigeria. It seemed that from 1962 to 1969 everybody's world became wider, whether the moral capacity to cope with it was there or not. There is a stage in moral development that calls upon us to decide how we are going to view the world and the challenges presented by those unresolved issues that make the eleven o'clock news every night.[2]

We, as trained ministers, must be about widening our ministry beyond traditional upbringings. The Lord wants His church to be effective and to broaden itself beyond the local mission circle.

Adequate buildings and space for migrant child care is limited in North Carolina. Saint James strives to do its best in contributing as much as possible towards this extended ministry among the migrant community, for example, the church allows the Head Start program to utilize the building free of charge. This helps the church to make up "In-Kind" dollars. When an organization receives federal funds, the agency must supplement 25% of the total grant with non-federal dollars. Church members also volunteer their time in the child

---

[2]Samuel D. Proctor, Samuel Proctor: My Moral Odyssey, (Valley Forge, PA: Judson Press, 1989), 129.

care center. This also counts towards "In-Kind" dollars. Much of the writer's time is spent ministering to the particular needs of migrant families, assisting with legal problems and directing parents to the appropriate community agencies which can administer to their needs. It is very helpful for the families to know that there is someone who cares. However, this caring for migrants can be terminated at any time by the grower.

> Whatever the migrant farmworker does is subject to the arbitrary veto of the grower. Rev. Jack Mansfield, for example, noticed that during the summer heat, workers were often sick at the end of the day. A doctor told him they should be taking salt tablets. Rev. Mansfield offered to furnish the tablets if the grower would supervise their daily distribution. (An overdose can be fatal.) The grower refused. He did not want to be bothered. Another migrant minister filed complaints about the conditions in one camp. Not only did the local authorities refuse to act, but later the minister was barred from the camp.[3]

Saint James hopes this "Model Of Ministry" will be a model that will interest other churches to do similar mission ministries. The church should not idly stand by when humankind is suffering economically and socially injustices. Dr. Martin Luther King, Jr., penned to his "Dear Fellow Clergyman" from the Birmingham Jail,

> Injustice anywhere is a threat to justice everywhere. But the judgment of God is upon the church as never before. If today's church does not recapture

---

[3]Truman Moore, The Slaves We Rent, (New York: Random House, 1965), 116.

the sacrificial spirit of the early church, it will lose its authenticity, forfeit the loyalty of millions, and be dismissed as an irrelevant social club with no meaning for the twentieth century. Every day I meet young people whose disappointment with the church has turned into outright disgust.[4]

The church is the new humanity, the body of Christ, the people of God who gather together for worship, fellowship, mission, evangelism, and education. It is through these tasks that the body of Christ is animated, the will of the divine head is done *in* the world, the influence of the new humanity spreads, and the responsibility of the people of God is rightly discharged.

The Church is God's primary agency for mission. The sees the church having the same mission as that of the Lord. The church is carrying out the mission of Christ Himself.

"As my Father hath sent me, even so I send you" (Jn. 20:21b). The mission ministry of the church is to make Jesus Christ known by presenting the gospel to all people of the world with the purpose of bringing a healing to the broken humanity.

In order to be effective, the church must model what society (family and community) should be, rather than critique what it is not. The church has a responsibility to remind the institutions of their obligations to dispense justice to this hostile humanity. The church must not be guilty of telling others what they are not doing, and failing to do what it is supposed to be doing. The church should be educating itself on key issues, advocating social justice and human rights. Most churches seem to be doing an excellent job in taking care of its local mission. It seems that we take care of those that have taken care of us.

---

[4]Martin Luther King, Jr., Why We Can't Wait, (New York: The American Library, 1964), 92.

Christ's church mission is far beyond the local community, but a call to a global one.

> And if you lend to those from whom you hope to receive, what credit is that to you? Even sinners lend to sinners, to receive as much again. But love your enemies, and do good, and lend to sinners, to receive as much again. (Lk. 6:34-35 NAS)

Jesus affirms that one need not possess any special grace of generosity of spirit to be able to respond to people who are loving and good to us. Nor does it require a spirit of sacrifice or liberality to invest in people when we have assurance of receiving at least as much in return. Even sinners, i.e., anybody, can trade favor for favor.

The oppressed people must not be guilty of hating the oppressors. The Lord has called us to love the hostile and critical people much more than they deserve to be loved--this is grace. Jesus is removing our excuses for not having love for all humanity. When the church reaches out to needy families that come into the community with love, it illustrates that the church members are the sons and daughters of the Most High. The writer believes that a true child bears the character and inculcates the spirit of the parent.

To those who have been wounded by a society of social and economic injustice, the church must demonstrate God's love to a broken humanity. There may come a time when one wants to retaliate with violence. The people of God should have enough of His grace to be generous in forgiving those who have been injurious to them.

The church must be a fellowship of grace. It is central in the life of the church. Not only does God save us by grace, but He calls us together as His people by grace. We are to live our lives in grace, we are to be a gracious people. "And be kind to one another, tender hearted, forgiving one another..." (Eph. 4:32) But not even that is enough. We are to love one another as Christ loved us. "And walk in love, as Christ loved us and gave himself up for us, a fragrant offering and sacrifice to God" (Eph. 5:2). In these two admonitions we are at the ethical heart of our faith.

The church should be as one of those points of the world where the love of God is poured forth for the healing of our brokenness, where the grace of Christ overcomes our estrangement and alienation. Grace is the great reality, linking the Old and New Testament. The God of grace is active in both, but He expresses His grace most particularly in Jesus of Nazareth.

God called His Church into being, as He called Israel to be His people. The God of the Old Testament is the same as in the New Testament. He is the Father of our Lord Jesus Christ. The Apostle Paul tells how God loves the church.

> Husbands, love your wives, as Christ loved the church and gave himself up for her, that He might sanctify her, having cleansed her by the washing of water with the word, that He might present the church to himself in splendor, without spot, or wrinkle or any such thing, that she might be holy and without blemish. (Eph. 5:24-27)

These new people were aware that they had been called not because of their goodness and virtue, but by the grace of Christ. Only the grace of God could have seen anything good in them and made anything good out of them.

Christ redeemed them, setting them free, so they could be His people. It is the truth that they were not held in political bondage the way old Israel had been kept in Egypt. But had been imprisoned by the dark and sinister powers: sin and death. But Christ, through His death and resurrection, had set them free from both. "For the law of the Spirit of life in Christ Jesus has set me free from the law of sin and death." (Rom. 8:2)

Jeremiah had envisioned a new covenant. The old one had been external and too easily broken. In the new covenant, God would write His law, not upon tablets of stone, but upon their lives. Jesus enacted this new covenant when He instituted the Lord's Supper.

> This cup is the new covenant in my blood... (1 Cor. 11:24) God declared the church His new people. Peter said it like this:
>
> Once you were a no people, but now you are God's people; once you had not received mercy but now you have received mercy. (1 Pet. 2:10)

Our church mission must go beyond the local parish. The task of mission is to see that the gospel's response to every human condition is implemented at the intersection where the Christian community meets the rest of the human family. God's mission for His church is His witnesses, ".."and unto the uttermost part of the earth." (Acts 1:8)

This **"Model in Ministry"** which addresses and serves the needs of migrant children and their families will suggest to congregations that the church should never "not do" mission ministry. The church should place a strong emphasis upon identifying the mission needs. There are more needs existing in every church community than any church can adequately meet. The church must be informed of its resources in doing mission. This is why the model ministry suggests that the church should take resourceful people within the congregation, expanding its mission ministry. In some churches, there are bankers, lawyers, doctors, accountants, school teachers, certified public accountants, maintenance engineers, college professors and presidents. This gives more reasons for expanding mission ministry. If these people can manage thousands of dollars, and write grants for the secular community, why not utilize these same talents within the churches, in the name of Christ? The resourceful people within the church would not have to leave their jobs, but through training workshops, they may be better equipped to execute a broader ministry for the church. Clodovis Boff and Leonardo Boff in their book, Liberation Theology, indicate:

> With the arrival of the theology of liberation on the contemporary scene, theology is no longer for theologians alone. Now it involves whole people of God, clergy and laity alike.

Theology has become genuinely and truly ecclesial.[5]

---

[5]Clodovis Boff and Leonardo Boff, Liberation Theology, (San Francisco, CA: Harper & Row, Publishers, 1986), 1.

4

THE LIFE-STYLE OF A MIGRANT FARMWORKER

Who Are These People?

Migrants are people with agricultural skills and abilities who make significant contributions to the economy of our day. "Migrant families usually are very poor. The average income of a migrant family of two is just over $3,000 per year."[1] They are people of dignity and worth. Migrants deserve a caring ministry of love, a ministry in which the church is aware of hunger, housing, and health needs. Who can do this better than the pastor and his/her congregation?

The four primary groups of the migrant population are:

    a. Blacks

---

[1]Cecil D. Etheredge, Migrants, (Atlanta, Georgia: Baptist Convention, 1985), 5.

b. Haitians

c. Hispanics

d. Whites

Migrant farmworkers make up a small but important subgroup of the domestic hired work force. According to the Federal Register,

> A migrant family, means for the purpose of Head Start eligibility, a family with children under the age of compulsory school attendance who change their residence by moving from one geographic location to another, either interstate or intrastate, within the past twelve months, for the purpose of engaging in agricultural work that involves the production and harvesting of tree and field crops and whose family income comes primarily from this activity.[2]

Year after year migrant farmworkers come to North Carolina by the thousands looking for employment. This is illustrated in the 1992 Estimate Of Migrant And Seasonal Farmworkers During Peak Harvest By County. (See Appendix A). The migrant farmworkers are most likely to be transported by their labor contractors. Migrant farmworkers, whose children we have served, describe their work as very stressful, back-breaking, with long hours and low pay. There is always an uprooted life-style that has very little sense of home. Migrant workers say little about their living and working conditions. The contributions of migrants may seem small in one sense,

---

[2]Department Of Health And Human Services, Administration Of Grants, Federal Regulations, Title 45 Part 1305.2 (1), (Washington, DC: Office Of The Secretary, Office Of Grants And Procurement, 1992), 152.

yet, they make a major contribution to the agricultural market to the United States. Without their low cost labor, vegetables and fruits would not be available at a reasonable price. If migrant farmworkers were not utilized, who would plant and harvest the crops and at what cost?

> Migrant labor harvest many of the crops on North Carolina's 65,000 farms. North Carolina crops are harvested by migrant labors. Both growers with large farm operations and those with small farm operations hire migrant laborers. Where do the workers come from? And who would harvest the tobacco, cucumbers, tomatoes, apples, and other produce with them? These questions were asked of growers throughout the state. Alvin Stepp, an apple grower in Henderson County, responded, What would I do without migrant labors? That I don't know.
>
> Migrants appear to be the only help available at this time. Our workers are from Mexico, and we've been working with the same people now for seven or eight years. I don't know what we' do without them.[3]

David Burbage, a farmer in Beaufort County said, "I could not get the work done without migrants. They are just as much a part of the farm as I am."[4] Mr. Burbage uses migrant workers to transplant tobacco, weed the fields, and I harvest the crop. Another farmer, Robert G. Warren, in Buncombe County

---

[3] John C. Brooks, "One Family's Success Story," Migrant Housing Bulletin, (Raleigh, North Carolina: NC Department Of Labor, Division Of Occupational Safety And Health, Bureau Of Migrant Housing, 1991), 2.

[4] Ibid.

states, "All we use are migrants. We'd shut down without them! Nobody else will work. Our local people are gone."[5]

In conversing with some migrant workers, the writer has been told that they have worked seven days a week and twelve hours a day. Some migrant worker have said that when working these long shifts they are allowed a half hour to rest, a cold sandwich and a pop for their meal. They have no place to wash the dirt and pesticide from their hands. There are no private toilets, which is more difficult for the women.

The crew leader/labor contractor is the mediator between the migrant farmworker and the crop owner. Often, the crew leader is the interpreter for both the migrant farmworker and the crop owner. The writer indicates that, in conversing with crew leaders, some were once migrant farmworkers themselves. They have worked their way through the ranks, and know all the tricks and trades of a dishonest crew leader. Many migrants say that the crew leaders/labor contractors forget quickly how life can be as a migrant farmworker. The crew leader has complete control over the migrant farmworker. He is the one who oversees all the transporting to the fields, to the market, and to the doctor. When the crops are ended, the crew leader is the one that transports the workers to their next destination. He finds shelter, and work for their survival. When the farmworkers have depleted their funds, it is the crew leader who loans them money. It has been evident in the course of serving migrant families, that parents express how they do not make enough money to manage their family's needs and are forced to live in indebtedness to the crew leader and others. One migrant farmworker has said,

> I always need the crew leader to talk between me and the farmer. In fact, I need him for everything.

---

[5]Ibid.

> He takes me to my new home: a rundown trailer shared by eight other men. In the kitchen there are lots of bugs because the door is broken and there no screens. When I get hungry I have to ask the crew leader for a ride to the store. He goes for me since I don't know any English yet. He overcharges me for the bread and potato chips he brings. I know I'm already increasing my debt, but you have to eat right?[6]

Migrant parents have shared their feelings of invisibility among the communities in which they reside. The migrant farmworkers have said that they and their family members often feel that the local communities would like them to leave. They are not well received.

> The superior group always treats the inferior in its first stages as being invisible. Ellison's book Invisible Man is so effective because he was not only telling the story of African people, and of people of color in the 1950's but he was giving an account of how America has turned us all into invisible people. In the Prologue the protagonist goes for a walk and walks into a White man and he does not even know that he has been bumped. (Ralph Ellison, 1972.) How many times have not we gone to a store or super market and as we stand there waiting to pay our bill the sales person ignores us; we feel totally humiliated. The violence of it all is that we are not even acknowledged as being present. The invisibility issue is a very serious one which

---

[6]Duke University Students through the Center for Documentary Studies, Migrant Summer: A Documentary View Of The Lives Of Migrant Farmworkers In North Carolina, (Research Triangle Park, North Carolina: PBM Graphics, 1991), 18.

constantly affects students of color on campuses. Often there are no courses, no professors, no one in the administration from their background.[7]

The writer recalls how people from New York and New Jersey used to talk about how things were much better there, than in the southern states. Several Duke University students documented accounts as to their relationship to the crew leader experience.

> Someday a man offers me a chance to go north, to a place where there is plenty of work for everyone. $4.00 an hour - that's a lots of money in Mexico. I know how to work in the fields, that's no problem. In my mind I can picture the house and food that I will get (free, he says) after a long day making a lots of money working in these fields. I think about my children, how happy they will be to receive money from me, to be able to eat okay. So I take this chance. What could I lose? I have a little money saved up to pay a •coyote,• the guy who sneaks you across the border. Then the crew leader picks a whole bunch of us up in his van. It is a long ride crowded into the back of a van and we are constantly afraid of being stopped by "La Migra" (immigration police). After a couple days, we get to North Carolina. I knew it would be tough not to know English. But it really hits you, you really feel it, when you get to this state and everyone here speaks only English, and all the signs on the road and the voices on the radio are in English. It's like they don't want to see you

---

[7]David T. Abalos, "Multicultural And Gender Inclusive Education In The Service Of Transformation" (keynote address, Seton Hall University, 1990), 15.

there either. But your hands and back and legs are perfectly okay, so long as you put them to good use working for the grower "el ranchero." Pretty soon I find out that I am already in debt-- owe the farmer $90.00 for the trip up. I'm not sure that is right because the farmer doesn't speak Spanish. I always need the crew leader to talk between me and the farmer.[8]

The Role Of A Crew Leader/Labor Contractor

The crew leader in the migrant community is the means of survival for the farmworker. The crew leader has to acquire an application for a permit to become a "Farm Labor Contractor" from the Employment Security Commission before he/she can operate in that county. An Application For A Labor Contractor can be obtained from any office of the Wage and Hour Division, United States Department of Labor, or any North Carolina Employment Security Office. The Employment Security Commission mails the application to Tallahassee, Florida. Wilson County issued 31 Farm Labor Contractor permits in 1992.

There were 40 Labor Contractor permits issued in Nash County in 1992. For both counties, 98% of these Farm Labor Contractors were Hispanics. The crew leader can be fined if he/she is caught in violation of the Farm Labor Contractor's law. There have been heavy fines placed upon crew leaders for being in violation of this law.

> Although crew leaders and their camps alternate between benevolence and despotism, the latter extreme is too easily reached or even crossed; as

---

[8]Duke University Students Through The Center For Documentary Studies, 17-18.

recently as 1983 several crew leaders in North Carolina were convicted for holding migrant farmworkers in conditions of slavery.[9]

The crew leader must have a "Farm Labor Contract." This means any person other than an agricultural employer, or an employee of an agricultural employer or agricultural association who, for any money or other valuable consideration paid or promised to be paid, reforms any farm labor contracting activity. "As an employer, a farm labor contractor would recruit, solicit, hire, employ, furnish, or transport any migrant or seasonal agricultural worker. "[10]

Employees have different opinions about the behavior of their crew leaders. Some will say that their crew leader's attitude is good, some may say it is ok, and others may say his/her attitude is very cruel.

> He was usually on the road with four to five months a year. During that time, he was the crew's official representative. It is the crew leader, nor the grower of the corporate farm, who is recognized as the employer. Whether or not a migrant ends the season money ahead or money behind often depends on the crew leader. Little Jim's crew was lucky he was honest. But not all crew leaders are like Little Jim. There are over 8,000 crew leaders in the migrant streams. They come in all shades of reliability and honesty. Good or bad, the few leaders perform a service that is available to the grower.

---

[9]Ibid., 12.

[10]W.E. Eickoff, Extension Agricultural and Resource Economics, "North Carolina Farm Labor Rules and Regulations", (Agriculture Extension Service - North Carolina State university, 1986), 11.

With one thing and another, Hamp cleared about $20,000 during a fair year. Some of it he spent on his own pleasures, same he put in the bank or in his own store in Florida. And every few years he brought another second-hand bus far the crew. Croaked as he was, Hamp lacked the cruelty of some crew leaders.[11]

Willard Barnes had a crew in a Long Island camp working in potatoes. When the time came for them to go South, one old woman in the crew was too sick to travel. Willard put off the trip for two days, but the old woman didn't get any better. So he just packed up the crew and left her. She awoke from a feverish sleep and saw the first flakes of snow falling.

She was alone in the camp in a drafty, unheated cabin. Certain that she was dying, the old woman bundled up and walked through the deserted camp in the light snow. In the evening she walked into the main street of a little suburban Long Island town and sat down on the corner.

When a Welfare Department worker found her, she was half covered with fresh snow. She had been looking for a place to die, and something about the corner reminded her of home.

Another crew leader, Horace Front, had a crew in North Carolina, but he had promised the grower a bigger one. While they were sitting out a rainy spell, Horace drove his bus back to Mississippi and got ten high school boys. None of them had any money,

---

[11]Moore, 26-27.

but Horace promised he'd take care of them. When he got back to camp in North Carolina, the crop still was not ready to pick. The boys went four days without eating. Conditions in the camp were getting dangerous, when the Welfare Department found out about it, they offered to obtain surplus food for the crew. As crew leader, Horace would have to certify that the crew was without work. But Horace had other ideas. He wanted the Welfare Department to let him have the food so that he could give it to the crew. He insisted that it would hurt his reputation *in* Florida if it became known that his crew had •to take off welfare.• It didn't seem to bother him that they were half starved.

What Horace wanted was to sell the food to the workers "on credit." When a case worker and a migrant minister checked on the camp, they found that Horace decided to feed the crew himself rather than back down.[12]

The crew leader/labor contractor is the person that communicates to the crop owner on behalf of his workers. The grower must make sure that the crew leader is in no violation of the law. The law states, "Before employing the services of a farm labor contractor, (crew leader) a potential employer should verify the following:

a. That the contractor has a valid certificate that is in full force from the United States Department of Labor and that is valid for the activity to be performed;

b. That the contractor has specific migrant labor authorization for use of his vehicles and housing;

---

[12]Ibid., 30-31.

> c. That the contractor maintains required vehicle insurance and uses only properly licensed drivers.[13]

For I was hungry, and ye gave me meat: I was thirsty, and ye gave me drink: I was a stranger, and ye took me in:" (Mt. 25:35) When the Christian Community fails to reach out to any broken humanity; it forces upon that particular people to hold on to the best close thing.

That leaves the migrant people no other choice but to cleave to their crew leaders.

> In fact, I need him for everything. He takes me to my new home: A run down trailer shared by eight other men...When I get hungry I have to ask the crew leader for a ride to the store. He goes for me.[14]

There are some decent and honest crew leaders. The people enjoy working for them.

> Little Jim was a good crew leader. His bus, the Beanpicker Special, was a little run-down, and the tires were slick....But not all crew leaders are like Little Jim....When he took out money for Social Security, he always turned it in, as he was supposed to....If there was a big shopping center on the way back from the field, he'd stop and let the crew do their shopping instead of in little stores near the camp, where they always overcharged.[15]

Over the past twelve years, the writer has seen much improvement between the grower, farm labor contractor and the farmworkers. Yet there is a great need and opportunity for the church to focus its ministry toward this community.

---

[13]Eickoff, 12.
[14]Moore, 26
[15]Ibid.

The labor contractor contracts with the crop owner to bring so many persons to harvest the crop at a certain price. The crew leader agrees on the time of arrival for the picking of the crops. He does not always get there on time, and sometimes he never gets there.

> For example, a farmer can make a simple agreement with a crew leader for a given number of migrants at a specified date.

> They will agree on a price, and the farmer, theoretically, can rest assured that his labor problems will be taken care of. In practice, however, the farmer can never rest easy until he sees the crew pull into camp. An unscrupulous crew leader can shift his crew to a higher-paying farm at the last minute. The first farmer can easily lose his crop for the lack of harvest laborers, Because both the migrants and the farmers depend on the crew leader, he is in a good position to take advantage of both…[16]

The crew leader/farm labor contractor is very important to the migrant worker; he/she is sometimes their only reliable friend. Migrant workers depend on their crew leader for many things towards their livelihood. Because of the diverse lifestyle of migrants and the people of the communities in which they work, it is often that the needs of migrant people are invisible to the immediate community. Although many of the community people cannot speak Spanish, to most migrant people a sincere smile and a warm acceptance would be welcomed more than one can imagine. The church can be

---

[16]Ibid., 27.

a role model in setting a friendly atmosphere towards the disenfranchised community.

Health Care Problems Among Migrants

Many migrants do not receive health care services. There are various reasons for the lack of health care among poor Americans. This "Model In Ministry" will focus on the lack of health care services among the migrant population.

According to the National Association of Community Health Centers, Inc:

> During the past quarter century, our nation's health care system has undergone tremendous growth in resource capacity, sophistication of medical technology, and insurance coverage of the formerly uninsured. The health care system has achieved major successes: Americans are living longer, infant mortality has dropped, and even such chronic diseases as hypertension are declining. But the significant progress achieved early in this period has nearly vanished in cent years, and gaps in access to care actually have widened.[17]

Approximately 10 to 15 percent of the population, depending on how medical underservice and its results are measured, are left behind. They include:

- Those who lack public or private insurance: More than 31 million fall into this category. Nearly half are from low-income families, and almost one-third are children.

---

[17]National Association Of Community Health Centers, Inc., "Access To Community Health care: A Critical Priority For The 1990's", (Position Paper, 1990), 1.

- Those who are underinsured: More than 53 million insured Americans are actually underinsured for important primary and preventive health services. Nearly 14 million women of child-bearing age are uninsured for obstetrical care.

- Those who live in areas with insufficient health care resources: In 1989, 33 million Americans were living in designated health manpower shortage areas, half in rural and half in urban areas.

- Those who face racial, cultural or language barriers to care: Long-time U.S. residents such as Native Americans and Blacks, as well as new arrivals such as Southeast Asians and Central Americans, report these problems.

- Those who are at high risk for health problems: These include high-risk pregnant women and their babies, migrant and seasonal farmworkers, homeless persons, substance abusers, and individuals with AIDS.

For more and more of these vulnerable populations, community based health programs have become the only source of entry level and ongoing primary health care.

Access to health care showed marked improvements from the 1950's to 1982; the gap between rich and poor was closing.

> Unfortunately, since 1982, the gap has widened. The widening gap is a function of maldistribution of resources, increasing lack of health insurance, and the growing reluctance of some health care providers to reach out or even to accept indigent patients.[18]

---

[18]Ibid.

Less than ten miles from Saint James Christian Church Child Care Center in Fountain, North Carolina, two medical centers closed their doors for services. The Saratoga, North Carolina Medical Center building was sold and hauled away. The Walstonburg, North Carolina Medical Center closed in 1989 and stayed closed until the Spring of 1991.

> During the 1980's, many traditional private sector providers have responded to the difficulties in the health care system by withdrawing from resource-poor communities or restricting services to certain population groups, Despite the overall increase in practicing physicians, isolated rural areas and economically deprived urban and rural communities have actually lost physicians.[19]

The Catholic Social Ministries, Rural Health Care and East Carolina University School of Medicine reopened the Walstonburg Medical Center from June through October so that migrant families would receive medical services. In 1991, staff from the Walstonburg Medical Center, reported that 91 migrants had been served by them. Migrants receiving health care services were from Wilson, Pitt, and Greene counties. This year, 1992, this health care provider served 170 migrants. The physicians were volunteers who desire to give something back to society.

The Nash County Regional Health Clinic serves migrant families employed in Nash county and in the western part of Wilson county. Many of the children of these families are served by the Saint James Christian Church Child Care Center in Bailey, North Carolina. This center is situated twelve miles

---
[19]Ibid.

from the Nash County Regional Health Clinic. The migrant health clinic in Nash county served over 2000 migrants in 1991 and in 1992. This clinic provides services for migrant families from May through November. The clinic administrator, one doctor, several nurses, and clerical personnel are employed to staff this facility by the Nash County Health Department and by the East Coast Migrant Health Project.

According to the administrator of the migrant clinic in Nash county, a breakdown of illnesses by age group were reported as follows:

Infants

Formula Intolerance Diaper Rash

Fever

Viral Infections Diarrhea Children

Ear Infections (otitis media) Upper Respiratory Infections

Adults

Pregnancy (family planning)

Muscle and Joint Pain

GI Problems (stomach) Skin Disorders Sexually

Transmitted Disease Dental

Children Impetigo Diarrhea

Adults 65 and Over Hypertension Diabetes

The Redlands Christian Migrant Association (RCMA) of Immokalee, Florida, met in Washington, District of Columbia, May 1990, with the National Association of Community Health Centers, Inc., concerning full support for re-authorization of the National Health Service Corps (NHSC) programs through

Fiscal Year 1993. This group requested support for legislative changes which would provide incentives such as a Community Health Fellowship Program to improve, to publicize, and to broaden the interest of individuals in the scholarship and loan repayment components of the program. Both organizations specified that priority be given to residents of underserved areas, to disadvantaged and minority students, and to others interested in primary care as well as persons committed to serving in underserved areas as recipients of the NHSC Scholarship and Loan Repayment awards.

The Saint James Christian Church wrote letters to its elected officials in Washington, District of Columbia. The letters asked the two Senators and Representatives to assist in acquiring more rural health care for children of poor families in North Carolina. In doing this, we can become advocates for political changes.

The church can be that role model in involving the community and different denominations in becoming advocates for social and economic changes. In order for the church to be effective, it must model what society (family and community) should be rather than criticize what it is not. The church has a responsibility to remind the institutions of their obligations to dispense justice. The church must know how to encourage those political forces that affirm justice and rightness, and how to oppose those that seek only manipulation. This does not mean being a naive pawn of a political party or candidate. The church should educate itself on key issues, advocating social justice and human rights.

To implement the biblical mandate of social concern, it is important that church members study significant social and community issues and confront the congregation with data.

The church members have the obligation to become active in efforts to bring reconciliation, relief, and reform. When the church takes on these roles it becomes God's presence, and agent for redemption in the world. "Evil persons do not understand the importance of justice, those who follow the Lord are much concerned about it." (Prov. 28:5) The lack of proper health care services to humankind is lack of justice. Only an evil person can turn his/her head to an unhealthy society. Jesus said, "They that are whole need not a physician; but they that are sick." (Lk. 5:31b NAS)

According to A Guide For Providing Social Services In Head Start:

> The Head Start program is based on the premise that children living in poverty are subject to risks to and unintentional neglect of their health, education, and welfare. From the time of conception, the social and economic disadvantages of poverty have their effect on the child, because health services are usually inadequate and often inaccessible. Experiences are necessarily limited, so that the young child is often handicapped in his ability to communicate, and is frequently stifled in his desire to learn. Head Start is viewed as an opportunity to intervene in the developmental process in such a way as to insure that the children enrolled in the program, and their families, receive the services necessary to their positive growth and development.[20]

---

[20]Kellene U. Bruce, Project Director, A Guide For Providing Social Services In Head Start, (Washington, District of Columbia: Associate, Control, Research and Analysis, Inc., 1980), 1.

Educational Background Of Migrants

The writer recommends that churches consider using available space for community involvement programs. What we have done at Saint James Christian Church is make available some of our unused space for the ministry to migrant people. We have initiated classes for migrant parents. Every Tuesday and Thursday at the Fountain center we have English as a Second Language Classes [ESL] and GED classes. Monday, Wednesday and Friday the same classes are taught at the Bailey center. The Fountain center is supported by Pitt Community College, and the Bailey center is supported by Nash Community College. Saint James has also started a "Family Literacy Project." This project is housed in a mobile unit that visits both day care centers. The mobile unit is in Fountain on Tuesday and Thursday, and in Bailey on Monday, Wednesday and Friday. The Literacy Project is funded by East Coast Migrant Head Start Project, Arlington, Virginia, and the Administration for Children Youth and Families [ACYF) Washington, District of Columbia.

These educational programs for migrants, afford the magnificent opportunities for any individuals who come in contact with the children. Many of our staff have taken advantage of sharpening their skills in the class room, and working with computers. The aim for the Family Literacy Project is to allow families interaction to encourage greater educational success for the children. The mobile unit has served five counties in the eastern part of North Carolina, Nash, Wilson, Pitt, Greene and Wayne counties. Our program offers babysitting for the students' children during the hours parents are attending classes. This "Model in Ministry" hopes to encourage other churches and organizations to become involved in community services programs.

Before proceeding with any community service program, churches and organizations must complete a needs assessment of that community. First, one must establish that there is a need, and that there are people who are willing to give assistance. Second, a building evaluation is needed; Is the facility equipped to handle this project?

The majority of migrants have very little education. Because of this, the migrant farmworker's greatest desire is for their children to gain the best education offered and learn how to speak English.

> Most hired farmworkers (56 percent) have not graduated from high school, only 16 percent of all wage and salary workers. In fact, a third of all hired farmworkers have completed less than 9 years of school. Conversely, only 13 percent of hired farmworkers have had some college experience, versus 45 percent of all wage and salary workers.[21]

For hired farmworkers in the United States for the year of 1990, the years of schooling completed varied significantly by racial/ethnic group:

> Hispanics had lower educational levels than Whites, Blacks, and others. Only 13 percent of all Hispanics, for example, had completed high school versus 60 percent of all White hired farmworkers and 40 percent of Blacks and others hired. Almost three quarters (72 percent) of the Hispanics had completed less than 9 years of school and 30 percent were functionally illiterate, that is, had completed less than 5 years of schooling. Hispanics

---

[21] Victoria J. Oliveira, "A Profile Of Hired Farmworkers, 1990 Annual Averages", (Agriculture Economic Report No. 658, 1990), 4.

had a median educational level of only six years, while Blacks and others had completed 10 years, and Whites 12 years.[22]

A survey was expedited by Saint James Christian Church. The results reported were from 34 Adult migrant farmworkers who were heads of household. There were nine people grades 0-5, 16 people grades 6-9, 5 people grades 10-11, and 4 people grade 12. There were none above grade 12.

According to a manual written by Carolyn Corrie, Into the Fields,

> Migrant children lag far behind their peers in level of education; U1e people in developing nations; and barriers of language and lack of transportation prevent many farmworkers from obtaining the basic services they need. surely, it seems, a group of energetic, caring and capable students can offer significant help to improve these situations. In turn, clearly, most colleges and universities provide too few opportunities for their: students to engage in 'real world,' hands on, experiential learning.[23]

It is not just the college and university students that lack this kind, of experience, but there are people on our church pews who fall in this same category. There is a need for education among the migrants. Knowledge gives people power, and this is lacking in the migrant population.

When working with the migrants, one must remember that the teacher-student relationship is a reciprocal process. Just

---
[22]Ibid.

[23]Carolyn Corrie, Into the Fields: A Guide and Resource Manual for Student Initiatives with Farmworkers, (Durham, North Carolina: Center for Documentary Studies at Duke University, 1991), 45.

as the migrant is willing to learn English, the non-migrant should be willing to learn conversational Spanish. A wise teacher always learns from his/her students. A multicultural educational program is the key to migrant ministry. We all have something to contribute in the educational process. The Spanish word "mestizaje" means the coming together of cultures and civilizations that are in no way antagonistic to each other, but that enrich each other. The more familiar we are with one another, the more we can learn from each other. Do we have the opportunity to tell about ourselves, and get to know the other self? Leslie Marmon Silko begins her novel, Ceremony, by telling us about the importance of stories.

> I will tell you something about stories. (he said).
>
> They aren't just entertainment. Don't be fooled. They are all we have, you see, all we have to ward off illness and death. You don't have anything if you don't have stories. So they try to destroy the stories let the stories be confused or forgotten. They would be happy. Because we would be defenseless then.
>
> He rubbed his belly. I keep them here. (he said). Here, put your hand on it. See, it is moving. There is life here for the people.[24]

This is an extraordinary statement of how all men and women are pregnant with the stories of their lives; every person, regardless of the racial/cultural background they come from, have within them a sacred self. Our sacred self must be born as Elaine Pagels tells us, quoting from the gospel of St. Thomas,

---

[24]Leslie Marmon Silko, Ceremony, (New York: Penguin Books, 1979), 2.

Jesus Said "If you bring forth what is with you, what you bring forth will save you. If you do not bring forth what is within you, what you do not bring forth will destroy you."[25] This is what the writer hopes that will come forth in migrant educational ministry, that a greater appreciation for others and a continuation of the stories being told. The teacher can become a positive advocate for the migrant population. The stories of people of color must be heard. Multicultural education must be a priority in order to minister to the migrant population.

Jesus, the founder of our faith, can be viewed as the greatest example of multicultural leadership of all times. He became so much a part of other ethnical/cultural groups that his handpicked disciples were amazed. Remember the woman of Samaria that came to Jacob's Well to draw water? She was amazed that this man, being a Jew, allowed himself to have a conversation with a Samaritan woman. There was a time when Jesus' disciples wanted him to chase away the woman of the Syrophoenician community. He even goes home with a Pharisee for dinner, and a woman of the street came and washed his feet with her tears and wiped them with her hair. The Pharisees claimed if he was who he said he was, he would not have allowed this woman near him. Jesus reached out to the poorest of the poor, the loneliest of the lonely, and the most unacceptable people of His time so that He could minister to the needs of all humankind.

---

[25]Elaine Pagels, The Gnostic Gospels, (New York: Random House, 1979), XV.

5

A PASTORAL CARE APPROACH TO MIGRANT MINISTRY

Migrants seldom experience a sustained or continuing ministry. Thus, pastoral care, as we know it through the church, is unknown to many migrant people. Often their religious experience is no more than a brief encounter with clergy and/or lay people of the church which allows little depth in Christian relationships.. A large percentage of the migrant population speaks only Spanish. The majority of the clergy in the United States are not bilingual. This closes the door to pastoral care. The church can open its doors to a Hispanic ministry. There are a few churches that have started a mission church for migrant families. This is one way of utilizing the unused space in our churches.

These are the basic problems encountered in the pastoral care of migrants. Migrants have great needs; Crisis is a daily encounter. Some church members make the excuse that the cultural gap between the migrant and the average middle-class person is so wide that few can bridge the gap to build a trust relationship. Jesus did not allow this to become an excuse for him not to care for people. The following story is sufficient for a caring ministry:

> And they came to Jericho: and as he went out of Jericho with his disciples and a great number of people, blind Bartimaeus, the son of Timaeus, sat by the highway side begging. And when he heard that it was Jesus of Nazareth, he began to cry out, and say, Jesus, thou son of David, have mercy on me. And many charged him that he should hold his peace: but he cried the more a great deal, Thou son of David, have mercy on me. And Jesus stood still, and commanded him to be called. And they called the blind man, saying unto him, Be of good comfort, rise; he calleth thee. And he, casting away his garment, rose, and came to Jesus. And Jesus answered and said unto him, What wilt thou that I should do unto thee? The blind man said unto him, Lord, that I might receive my sight. And Jesus said unto him, Go thy way; thy faith hath made thee whole. And immediately he received his sight, and followed Jesus in the way. (Mk. 10:46- 52)

Jesus refused to let any gap come between himself and the blind beggar. Jesus took time *to* talk with him and let him know that he was somebody. Jesus did not assume that he knew the man's problem. He asked for his request, "what wilt thou that I should do unto thee?" (Mk. 10:51) This may have been the only time that anybody seemed to care for the blind beggar's needs. Jesus allowed Blind Bartimaeus, the beggar, to:

Express his Experiences:

I feel like a nobody!

Express his Behaviors:

They have no respect for me as a person!

Express the Effects:

The lack of respect makes me feel depressed!

Often, we fail in pastoral care when we do not seek from people what their needs are. We fail to listen to our client's experiences, behaviors, and effects. We find in the migrant community that many experience rejection and denial. This can range from indecent housing, improper health care, *to* unfair wages and the list continues. To be effective in our pastoral care to migrants, we must first consider that the migrant population snot emotionally different from any other people. Only trust, a loving concern, and honesty will remove many barriers that block effective pastoral care. This will leave the door open for future pastoral care when the migrants return to the area. A true and lasting friendship can then be established between the church and the migrant family.

> Pastoral care has many levels of relationships.
>
> Christian pastors care for people on many different levels of relationship. At one and the same time, you may be the personal friend, next-door neighbor, pastor-preacher, pastor-counselor, and golf or fishing companion of the person to whom you I minister. Furthermore, you do not, unless you are a pastor in an unusually large city, spend much time with people who you never see again after finishing a series of three or four interviews. You are related to the same persons over a period of

years, during which your relationship moves from one level of formality and informality to another and back again, depending upon the variety of crises endured.[1]

The problems of migrant people include unemployment, food, clothing, housing, medical and dental care and transportation. Their lives are filled with vicious cycles. Poor employment means limited funds. Limited funds mean poor food and an inadequate diet. Poor food means poor health. Poor health means poor performance. Poor performance means poor employment, etc. Let us listen to the conversation of a migrant worker as she leaves Florida northbound on a crew leader's bus, Beanpicker." The bus has broken down beside the highway.

> They slept some (of us) in the bus, some on the roadside. The babies cried, and there was only warm soda to quiet them. Some of the crew had brought food: sandwiches, potted meat, and crackers. Others who had joined the crew only at the last moment were without either food or money. They had to wait until Little Jim (crew leader) was ready to feed them.[2]

Most migrants have known poor housing, little privacy, low self-image, no opportunity of pride ownership or pride in appearance, no sense of permanence. It is a constant struggle in trying to overcome something small when in deed it is something great. Psychological problems of feelings of isolation, inadequacy, anger, meaningless life and lack of long-term goals produce inefficiency and bitterness for these people.

---

[1] Wayne E. Oates, The Christian Pastor, 3d ed. ev., (Philadelphia: The Westminster Press, 1982), 190.
[2] Moore, 9.

Yet migrants continue to live in hope, that one day they can settle in a place which they can call home.

> At the edge of every town she looked at people rocking on their porches, watching the old bus go past. She wanted a place where you didn't have to move. Then she could watch people going by instead of always riding past somebody else's porch and seeing them sitting there. She could hang up her clothes in a closet, unpack all her bags and bundles. 'If I had a place like that,' she said, "I, wouldn't go to foot from the door. All this movin' round makes a body old."[3]

One cannot counsel migrant people by implementing the same methods used in suburbia or with the middle class. Migrants have immediate practical concerns. They do not see how "just talking about" a problem can help.

This does not mean that talking out a problem has no value to migrants. It does provide a release of emotions. It helps the counselor to understand the person's problem. It provides an opportunity for support. Some advice, specific suggestions, and practical help of a direct or material nature may be needed also. We, as pastors, must remember that our task is not to solve everybody's problems. There are times when we must counsel people in how to manage their problems.

The greatest attitude of the counselor is to be accepting, supportive, non-judgmental and compassionate. Nothing moves to the heart of a migrant quicker than the knowledge that someone has chosen to stand by him/her when crisis strikes. He/she knows firsthand the pain and suffering that injustice,

---
[3] Ibid., 11.

cruelty, prejudice and apathy can cause. One who chooses to stand by to bring relief becomes a friend. Saint James Christian Church has stood by and become a friend to many migrant families.

6

THE DELEGATE AGENCY

Saint James Christian Church began with one center that operated for six weeks. Saint James now operates two child care centers. The centers served one hundred eighty-six migrant children for seven months last year.

The administrative staff, component staff, and contextual associates have been instrumental in developing an Early Childhood Education Program that is of high quality and excellence. Our teachers, child care assistants, and other support personnel are well-trained and qualified. Saint James Christian Church aims to enhance greater productivity for local growers who employ migrant farmworkers. Both parents are able to work and thus provide additional income for their family. The children are no longer susceptible to unintentional abuse/neglect situations. The Centers are available for English as a Second Language {ESL} and G.E.D. classes, training events, and community meetings. Saint James encourages and coordinates these efforts. Our success has been, and is being realized daily. The children are healthier and happier. Parents have confidence in our programs; therefore, they are supportive. In addition, for children who go on to public schools, the transition is smoother-less stressful for the child. As expressed by Ms. Jean Darden, Chapter One Director/Migrant Director, of the Greene County Public Schools

> If more migrant children could receive assistance and positive learning experiences before they enter public schools, frustrations would greatly decrease and retention would greatly increase.[1]

Saint James Christian Church intends to assure that services are provided for Migrant families and children who have the most serious need for Head Start services. As is the case throughout our Centers, one of our most paramount concerns is to provide individualized, developmentally appropriate, and multicultural programs for migrant children, including those who need specialized care--such as those who have disabilities. To qualify for services, children and their families must have moved during the past twelve months, meet poverty income guidelines, and be in pursuit of agricultural work. Throughout our centers, continuity of Head Start services is vital for these children as they move along the East Coast.

Saint James' enrollment at both centers is 241 migrant children 0-5 years. The majority of the children served are ages three or younger. The hours of operation are Monday through Friday from 6:00 A.M. until 6:00 P.M. Efforts are made to ensure that 85% of the children enrolled are in the Centers on a daily basis.

---

[1] Ms. Jean Darden, interview by Frances Batiks, Telephone interview, Bailey, North Carolina, 16 March 1992.

Saint James Christian Church assures that program enrollment opportunities are available to children with disabilities. Disabled children will be enrolled in the full range of Head Start services and activities in mainstream setting as well as receive needed special education and related services. Ten percent of the enrollment is children with disabilities.

Saint James Christian Church urges migrant parents to become actively involved in decision making regarding the program and the development of activities they consider helpful. Parents participate in the classroom as paid employees, volunteers, and observers. Parents participate in adult activities which they plan themselves. Parents, as prime educators, work with their own children, along with the support of the Head Start staff.

Saint James encourages parents to join the Head Start center staff in making decisions about content and operation of the program and how they and their child will participate in it.

Parents more readily participate if the activities that suit their own tastes and needs. Parent participation in the design of the Head Start program supports the program's success.

Parents who visit and work in the classroom have a better understanding of what the center is doing for their children and of the assistance their children may need at home.

The migrant family ministry has allowed Saint James Christian Church to become an ecumenical ministry. The Catholic, Baptist, Presbyterian, and Churches of Christ are working together in a shared ministry. We have two local dentists who provide on-site dental services for migrant children. There is a pediatrician from the East Carolina School of Medicine who visits and provides medical services. The dentists and pediatricians are members of our Health Services Advisory Committee. This committee consists of professionals from the health community. Center staff also schedule appointments for family members of our children for necessary medical and health care services with these professionals as well.

The migrant ministry has given the church a profound understanding of what outreach ministry is. Saint James Christian Church (Disciples of Christ) understands that the ministry of Jesus Christ is caring for humankind in spite of conditions and environment.

At the 1989 General Assembly of the Christian Church (Disciples of Christ) in the United States and Canada held in Indianapolis, Indiana, Saint James was given special recognition for its ministry. On this occasion, the Department of Homeland ministries recognized five churches for their 'Congregation Renewal Community Ministry.' At this time, Saint James also received another award from the Department of Reconciliation that read, 'Reconciliation Poverty Program.'

7

THE GRANTEE AGENCY

East Coast Migrant Head Start Project (ECMHSP) was initiated in May, 1974 to provide continuity of Head Start services to the children of migrant farmworkers on the east coast of the United States. The recipients are infants, toddlers, and preschoolers, sometimes as young as two weeks of age. ECMHSP arranges for the availability of Head Start services to these children primarily by contracting with existing agencies capable of providing the Head Start services (who then become ECMHSP delegate agencies), by operating its own center based program as training/technical assistance site in Florida, and by offering assistance to these agencies through the services of the Program Development Specialists. ECMHSP's work is supported by funds provided by the Migrant Programs Branch of the Administration for Children, Youth and Families of the Department of Health and Human Services.

The East Coast Migrant Head Start Project Corporation is a private non-profit agency whose members are delegate agencies who receive grant funds in the current fiscal year. These delegate agencies nominate and elect the ECMHSP Board of Directors which has legal and fiscal responsibility for ECMHSP.

The East Coast Migrant Head Start Project Parent Policy Council participates in the process of making decisions about the nature and operation of the program working in cooperation with the ECMHSP Board of Directors and ECMHSP's Executive Director.

The parents of each delegate agency are represented on the Council by an elected parent: the Council also includes representation from local communities.

The Administrative Office for ECMHSP is located in Arlington, Virginia, and is staffed by the Executive Director, Director Of Program Operations, Program Staff and Fiscal Staff. The Program Development Manager supervises the Regional Program Development Specialists who provide ongoing on-site training and technical assistance to the delegate agencies, in all program component areas, and provides valuable resources and guidance for program development within the total ECMHSP system. The center based ECMHSP Florida Branch administratively located in Winter Haven, Florida, operates center sites serving migrant infants, toddlers and preschooler. These service sites are also utilized for developing model programs available for replicating and training. ECMHSP is a multi-cultural program serving a majority pf its population under the age of three. Families served are approximately 85% Spanish-speaking; 10% are Black or Haitian and 5% White. To qualify for services, children must be five years or younger, fall within the poverty guidelines and have traveled or moved with their family within the past twelve months doing agricultural work.

ECMHSP, in the effort to provide outreach and continuity of service to the children of migrant farmworkers, has developed a systematic approach to the delivery of services. All centers funded by ECMHSP deliver services supporting all six components of the Head Start Project:

- Education--a quality individualized child development program.
- Health--limited medical, dent l, and mental health services.
- Nutrition--two or three nutritionally balanced meals and snacks daily funded by U. S. Department of Agriculture.
- Social Service--enabled parents to become aware of the local community services and resources available and facilitate their use.
- Parent Involvement--involved the parents in the development of their own children, in decision-making as members of the Center Committee and as representatives to ECMHSP's Parental Policy Council.
- Handicap Effort--a program mandated to recruit and serve children with handicapping conditions (10% of its funded enrollment).

To assure the quality of this service delivery system, ECMHSP maintains a staff of training and technical assistance professionals who provide consistent and personal guidance on-site to the program.

- When children leave a center funded by ECMHSP, their families are provided with Developmental and Health Continuity Records that portray the I health and developmental status of the child as ascertained by medical professionals and professional developmental assessment tools. These records are continually updated as the children receive individualized care in different centers. The programs continually educate the families as to the importance of maintaining Continuity Records.

- The records of all children served by ECMHSP were maintained *in* the Project's central office in Arlington, Virginia. These records are then available upon request to all delegate agencies. Presently, the grantee agency is providing training to the delegate agencies on a computerized record system. This system allows the delegate agencies to send and receive child-family data within minutes.

- Communication from the central office to the delegate agencies also serve as an outreach function guaranteeing continuity of care. For example, if a child with a severe handicapping condition, such as cancer, left Florida for eastern North Carolina, the centers in that area would be informed and directed to search actively for that child.

- Finally, all staff of ECMHSP are encouraged to support all efforts to assure continuity of care for migrant children and their families not only within the ECMHSP system but also, as possible, in areas where ECMHSP does not serve.

The goals of ECMHSP are as follows:

1. To provide continuity of Head Start services for migrant children on the east coast of the United States freeing parents from the emotional strain inherent in having unattended children in the fields and enabling children to develop their full human potential.

2. To provide Head Start services (an individualized developmental multicultural program for migrant children 0-5 years) by:
   - Association with already existing programs that can provide Head Start services;
   - Direct administration of model Head Start sites for migrant children;
   - Purchasing spaces for children in already existing programs; (These services were provided without duplicating already existing services in any way.)
3. To provide Head Start services to migrant children with handicapping conditions--at least 10% of the total population.
4. To continue to discover new ways for migrant children parents to become deeply involved in decision-making about the program and the development of activities they consider helpful and important in meeting their particular needs and conditions.
5. To provide on-going, on-site training and technical assistance to centers staff thus assuring the continual development of quality programming.
6. To provide paraprofessional staff with opportunities to develop professionally to the limit of their interests and skills.
7. To provide a system of programmatic and fiscal accountability.
8. To coordinate health services with the Migrant Health Projects and Rural Health Projects in order to provide comprehensive health services to migrant children and their families.

9. To establish linkages with other Migrant Programs Branch grantees and other community agencies to ensure that records will be transferred and programs will be coordinated to promote the development of children.

10. To act as a catalyst among health, educational, social service agencies, and religious organizations previously untapped for the Head Start program.

8

THE EVALUATION PROCESS

Saint James Christian Church is assessed annually by East Coast Migrant Head Start Project (ECMHSP). The Program Assessment entails observation, interview and document review. assesses its programs for the following reasons:

- To comply with federal regulations for funding and program evaluation;

ECMHSP

- Because the 70.2 REQUIRES parents to evaluate programs;
- To recognize staff's efforts;
- To share information about the program with staff, parents, and ECMHSP Arlington Office;
- To ensure the quality of care and services that children and families receive; and

- To identify areas that need improvement and new areas for future program development.

The parents are expected to conduct an assessment on the program prior to the ECMHSP Program Assessment. This year it was mandated that the program also be assessed by a community representative. The assessors use a checklist to evaluate each Head Start component (Administration, Education, Social Services, Parent Involvement, Continuity, Nutrition, Health, Disabilities, and Transportation). The Program Assessment Checklists are in English and Spanish.

During the assessment process, the Personnel Policy Manual and Job Descriptions are reviewed by the assessors, in order to ensure that management systems are implemented effectively in the program.

The fiscal operation of the program is audited twice a year by the ECMHSP Internal Auditor and annually by an Independent Certified Public Accounting Firm.

9

APPROACHING THE 21ST-CENTURY

Decent Housing For Migrants

Migrants are a population faced with serious problems. Many face hardships such as toxic drinking water, malnutrition, low education and income levels, and poor health care. Migrants focus most of their energy on surviving today, not on planning for tomorrow. For many, housing is a luxury item and decent housing may be inconceivable.

Unfortunately, providing housing for migrant people, is usually a low or non-existent priority for government and migrant groups. The difficult question is: How can decent housing be provided for migrant workers? The answer lies in gaining a better understanding of poor housing among the migrant community. Few communities support the development of migrant or seasonally operated housing, regardless of the importance of agriculture in the area. The not in my backyard mentality seems to be magnified when farmworkers are involved. While community approval may not be a paramount consideration in the minds of those seeking to develop the housing, it will certainly become an issue when zoning, subdivision, and construction approvals are needed.

There are three areas we need to look into for the 21st century concerning decent housing for migrant populations.

1. The need for greater public awareness of the plight of migrant workers.

2. The need for more technical assistance to housing developers to create affordable and supportive housing for migrant workers.

3. And the need to create and reform local, state and federal programs that can improve living conditions for migrant farmworkers.

Increased Appropriations

1. Increase appropriations for housing for migrant farmworkers, with special emphasis for those who are elderly and disabled.

2. In order to adequately serve migrant farmworkers, nonprofit housing sponsors need adequate resources for staff and management both during the development phase and after projects actually go into operation. HUD and FmHA should provide adequate resources at all phases of development and operation so that nonprofit organizations are encouraged to provide services to migrant farmworkers.

3. Congress should hold hearing forums on issues affecting active, migrant farmworkers, especially related to housing and federal benefits.

Research and Data

1. Because of the very limited data available on migrants, and the level and extent of housing needs, the Secretary of Agriculture and the Bureau of the Census should target research on the needs of this population.

2. A "Rural Homeless initiative should be established to finance nonprofit organizations to build and operate temporary housing for migrant workers and their families during the migrant season and for other rural homeless during the rest of the year.

3. Rural areas need technical assistance and training. The Farmers Home Administration (FmHA) should provide comprehensive training for the following groups' subject area:

    - A nonprofit developer and sponsor of migrant farmworkers' housing on all phases of housing development;

    - homeowners and building crew personnel on proper maintenance and minor repair of home, mechanical, and electrical systems;

    - FmHA staff in targeted state and district offices on farm labor, housing grant and loan programs, and the process for grants on loan approval and support.

Accountability

1. Benefits programs such as Supplement Security Income (SSI), food stamps and housing assistance, should conduct outreach to older, disabled migrants, and seasonal assistance in a timely manner. Special efforts should be made to eliminate language barriers to allow full participation in these programs.

2. In order to ensure the efficiency and timely processing of housing grants on loan applications, time limits should be imposed on FmHA for completion of certain actions, including pre-application, application review, environmental assessment, and appraisals.

3. For future development efforts, FmHA and Housing Urban Development (HUD) should encourage the use of housing designs which are more sensitive to family social structures, good management and upkeep, and supportive social services.

Improvements For The 21st-Century

We, the members of Saint James Christian Church endorse education and prevention for migrant populations, and urge health care providers to explore creative models of care in order to create real change in this population's health status.

Increased Public/Professional Awareness

1. Increase to at least 75 percent the proportion of primary care providers to migrant and seasonal farmworkers who provide their patient with culturally sensitive screening, counseling and immunization services.

2. Increase to at least 50 percent the proportion of primary care providers who use office reminder systems and client tracking systems to enhance their performance and follow-up of clinical preventive services.

Improve Services

1. Launch a national campaign for patient education to be implemented in 100 percent of the migrant health programs receiving Section 329 funds, which will include:

    a. Use children as agents of change.

b. Provision of appropriate audiovisual materials for health center's use with their patient populations.

c. Establish standardized clinical indicators which define and measure the impact of patient education.

d. Place special program priority on prevention and health education services.

e. Use lay health advisors in the provision of appropriate education services.

f. Mobilize resources for the development and delivery of these services to migrant populations.

2. Increase to at least 30 percent the proportion of farmworkers who participate regularly in health promotion activities at the work place.

Reduced Risk Factors

Increase to at least 50 percent the proportion of people who have received, as a minimum within the appropriate interval, all of the screening and immunization services and at least one of the counseling services appropriate for their age, sex and risk status as recommended by the United States.

Preventive Services Task Force

1. Increase availability of basic level preventive health education materials for migrant and seasonal farmworkers on 100 percent of the areas recommended by the Office of Migrant Health and the U.S. Preventive Services Task Force to include:

    a. Transmission of contagious disease, i.e., Sexually Transmitted Diseases (STD), immunization information, parasites, hepatitis.

    b. Detection and management of chronic disease, including hypertension and diabetes.

c. Pesticide and environmental risk factors.
d. Stress and safety awareness.

CONCLUSION

In conclusion, the writer believes that Increased Public/Professional Awareness, Improved Services, Reduced Risk Factors, and a Preventive Services Task Force would greatly aid or facilitate in fulfilling the needs of one of America's most disadvantaged groups, migrant farmworkers. The measure of a just society is found in its treatment of the least fortunate among its members. As we approach the 21st-Century, the very young and the very old remain at the top of any list of our most disadvantaged and vulnerable citizens. Among occupational groups, farmworkers have always been severely disadvantaged. The "farmworkers" are a group of people who are often very much in need of help. They remain a group that has been mostly out of sight and out of mind. This phenomenon can and should be changed.

One overwhelming problem lies at the heart of this; the migrant workers need an advocate who is neither dependent on the grower or the crew leader. There is no accountability to protect them from financial exploitation, overwork, robbery by the crew leader and poor, unhealthy housing provided. The Labor Department seems to have accepted these conditions as given and the scouting is sadly in need of correction.

It is the writer's recommendation that a church consortium could serve the migrant farmworkers and their families by calling for such accountability.

APPENDIX

1992 ESTIMATE QF MIGRANT AND SEASONAL FARMWORKERS DURING PEAK HARVEST BY COUNTY

COUNTY	MIGRANT	SFW	OVER 150	SPANISH	H2A
Alamance	195	650	250	175	8
Alexander	75	1200	100	75	0
Alleghany	150	400	75	150	0
Anson	25	175	200	25	0
Ashe	150	1000	20	150	0
Avery	250	400	10	250	0
Beaufort	480	650	320	450	0
Bertie	75	800	500	50	0
Bladen	600	2000	800	600	0
Buncombe	50	600	100	50	22
Brunswick	400	1400	600	400	0
Burke	40	1500	20	40	0
Cabarrus	20	650	100	20	0
Caldwell	25	200	100	25	0
Camden	105	130	235	0	0
Carteret	150	400	200	125	0
Caswell	295	900	200	295	12
Catawba	15	500	20	10	0
Chatham	100	300	200	100	36
Cherokee	40	600	75	40	0
Chowan	120	500	225	30	0
Clay	0	300	100	0	0
Cleveland	150	800	100	150	0
Columbus	550	1100	500	550	0
Craven	150	2100	300	125	26
Cumberland	275	650	500	200	0
Currituck	35	290	300	2	0

COUNTY	MIGRANT	SFW	OVER 150	SPANISH	H2A
McDowell	40	440	60	40	0
Macon	40	500	80	40	0
Madison	40	400	50	40	0
Martin	300	700	375	290	0
Mecklenburg	0	100	100	0	0
Mitchell	20	400	50	20	0
Montgomery	50	300	150	50	0
Moore	350	500	300	350	47
Nash	2150	1200	500	2000	0
New Hanover	75	275	125	75	0
Northampton	50	600	200	50	0
Onslow	350	400	125	350	14
Orange	290	375	200	290	0
Pamlico	100	400	150	90	0
Pasquotank	160	815	505	4	0
Pender	800	1600	1000	800	0
Perquimans	0	250	150	0	0
Person	425	1200	150	425	0
Pitt	2000	2000	1200	1975	0
Polk	50	300	80	50	0
Randolph	50	350	80	50	19
Richmond	300	400	325	300	76
Robeson	700	2000	1100	700	11
Rockingham	450	1000	300	400	247
Rowan	100	1170	200	100	0
Sampson	3500	1500	800	3200	31
Dare	0	0	0	0	0
Davidson	100	1000	100	100	6
Davie	25	300	100	25	8
Duplin	2500	1800	800	2200	147
Durham	75	350	50	75	32
Edgecombe	300	1100	400	300	20

APPENDIX

COUNTY	MIGRANT	SFW	OVER 150	SPANISH	H2A
Forsythe	500	1100	100	500	100
Franklin	300	2400	300	300	70
Gaston	50	200	10	50	0
Gates	10	300	150	10	0
Graham	0	250	50	0	0
Granville	300	2400	300	300	41
Greene	500	500	400	500	186
Guilford	350	700	350	275	38
Halifax	150	2000	250	150	0
Harnett	1000	1700	750	750	239
Haywood	60	800	150	60	0
Henderson	1500	2000	500	1200	0
Hertford	52	700	600	8	0
Hoke	30	200	150	30	0
Hyde	269	250	200	255	0
Iredell	100	1300	375	100	0
Jackson	50	550	75	50	0
Johnston	2000	1400	700	1750	63
Jones	150	700	150	125	0
Leo	325	450	250	325	87
Lenoir	400	800	600	400	158
Lincoln	350	1000	75	350	0
Scotland	20	220	150	20	0
Stanly	0	100	200	0	0
Stokes	550	1600	150	550	85
Surry	500	1400	250	450	30
Swain	25	200	15	25	0
Transylvania	50	300	75	50	0
Tyrrell	30	250	145	0	0
Union	0	100	350	0	0
Vance	150	1200	150	150	0
Wake	725	700	200	700	41

COUNTY	MIGRANT	SFW	OVER 150	SPANISH	H2A
Warren	50	1100	150	50	0
Washington	200	350	250	80	0
Watauga	50	700	20	50	0
Wayne	1100	1700	700	950	30
Wilkes	200	1500	400	150	0
Wilson	1300	350	300	1250	11
Yadkin	550	1500	150	550	42
Yancey	10	300	10	10	0
			TOTAL MIGRANTS:	33,304	33,896
			TOTAL SFW:	82,635	79,990
			TOTAL OVER 150 DAYS:	26.400	26,180
			TOTAL SPANISH:	30,110	31,029
			TOTAL H2A:		

BIBLIOGRAPHY LIST

Abalos, David T. *Latinas in the United States: The Sacred and the Political.* Notre Dame: University of Notre Dame Press, 1986.

Baff, Clodovis, and Leonardo Baff. *Liberation Theology.* San Francisco: Harper & Row Publishers, 1986.

Branch, Taylor. *Parting the Water: America in the King Years 1954-63.* New York, London, Toronto: Simon and Schuster, 1988.

Brooks, John C. "One Family's Success Story," *Migrant Housing Bulletin.* Raleigh, North Carolina: NC Department Of Labor, Division Of Occupational Safety And Health, Bureau Of Migrant Housing, 1991.

Bruce, Kellene U. *A Guide For Providing Social Services In Head Start.* Washington, District of Columbia: Associate, Control, Research and Analysis, Inc., 1980.

Bussmann, Claus. *Who Do You Say?.* Maryknoll, New York: Orbis Books, 1985.

Chopp, Rebecca S. *The Praxis of Suffering.* Maryknoll, New York: Orbis Books, 1986.

Cook, Michael. *Afro-American Literature in the Twentieth Century: The Achievement of Intimacy.* New Haven: Yale University Press, 1984.

The Comparative Study Bible. Grand Rapids, Michigan: Zondervan Bible Publishers, 1984.

Cone, James H. *God Of The Oppressed*. San Francisco, CA: Harpers & Row, Publishers, 1975.

Corrie, Carolyn. *Into the Fields: A Guide and Resource Manual for Student Initiatives with Farmworkers*. Durham, North Carolina: Center for Documentary Studies at Duke University, 1991.

Delgado-Horne, Asuncion. et. al. *Breaking Boundaries Latina Latina Writings and Critical Reading*. Amherst: University of Massachusetts Press, 1988.

Department Of Health And Human Services, Administration Of Grants, Federal Regulations. Title 45 Part 1305.2 (1). Washington, DC: Office Of The Secretary, Office Of Grants and Procurement, 1992.

Dorris, Michael. *Yellow Raft on Blue Water,* New York: Warner Books Inc., 1988.

Dubois, W. E. B. *The Soul of Black Folk*. New York: Signet Books, 1969.

Duke University Students through the Center for Documentary Studies. *Migrant Summer: A Documentary View Of The Lives Of Migrant Farmworkers In North Carolina*. Research Triangle Park, North Carolina: PBM Graphics, 1991.

Eickoff, W. D. Extension Agricultural and Resource Economics, "North Carolina Farm Labor Rules and Regulations." North Carolina: North Carolina State University, 1986.

Ellison, Ralph. *Invisible Man*. New York: Vintage Books, 1972.

Erikson, Erik. *Gandhi's Truth: On the Origins of Militant Nonviolence*. New York: W. W. Norton, ;1968.

Etheredge, Cecil D. *Ministry/Witness Resource Guide: Migrants.*

Atlanta, Georgia: Home Mission Board of the Southern Baptist Convention, 1985.

Gonzalez, Catherine G. and Justo L. Gonzalaz. *Liberation Preaching.* Nashville: Abingdon, 1980.

Gutierrez, Gustavo. *We Drink From Our Wells.* Maryknoll, New York: Orbis Press, 1984.

Kesey, Ken. *One Flew Over the Cuckoo's Nest.* New York: Signet Books, 1962.

King, Martin Luther, Jr. *Why We Can't Wait.* New York: The New American Library, 1964.

Lernoux, Penny. *Cry of the People.* Baltimore: Penguin, 1979.

Lewis, Oscar. *Five Families.* New York: New American Library, 1959.

Lightfoot, Sara Lawrence. *Balm in Gilead.* New York: Addison-Wesley Publishing Co., 1988.

Moore, Truman. *The Slaves We Rent.* New York: Random House, 1965.

Morales, Alejandro. *The Brick People.* Houston, Texas: Arte Publico Press, 1988.

National Association Of Community Health Centers, Inc. "Access To Community Health Care: A Critical Priority For The 1990's." Position Paper, 1990.

Oates, Wayne E. *The Christian Pastor.* Philadelphia: The Westminister Press, 1982.

Oliveira, Victoria J. "A Profile Of Hired Farmworkers, 1990 Annual Averages." Agriculture Economic Report, 1990.

Pagels, Elaine. *The Gnostic Gospels.* New York: Random House, 1979.

Proctor, Samuel D. *Samuel Proctor: My Moral Odyssey.* Valley Forge, PA: Judson Press, 1989.

Rivera, Edward. *Family Installments, Memories of Growing Up Hispanic.* New York: Penguin Books, 1983.

Schockley, John. *Chicano Revolt in a Texas Town.* Notre Dame: University of Notre Dame Press, 1974.

Scofield, D. D., Rev. C. I. *The Holy Bible.* New York: Oxford University Press, 1945.

Silko, Leslie Marmon. *Ceremony.* New York: Penguin Books, 1979. Simpson, Madden Janet and Sara Blake. *Emeraina Voices: A Cross Cultural Reader.* Forth Worth, Chicago, San Francisco: Holt, Rinehart and Winston, 1990.

Takaki, Ronald. *Strangers From a Different Shore.* New York: Little Brown and Co., 1989.

Walker, Alice. *The Color Purple.* New York: Pocket Books, 1982. Yezierska, Anzia. *Bread Givers.* New York: Persea Books, 1975.

www.ingramcontent.com/pod-product-compliance
Lightning Source LLC
LaVergne TN
LVHW051509070426
835507LV00022B/3013